W0254428

Exercises on the grammalogues and contractions of Pitman's shorthand - Primary Source Edition

J F. C Grow

Nabu Public Domain Reprints:

You are holding a reproduction of an original work published before 1923 that is in the public domain in the United States of America, and possibly other countries. You may freely copy and distribute this work as no entity (individual or corporate) has a copyright on the body of the work. This book may contain prior copyright references, and library stamps (as most of these works were scanned from library copies). These have been scanned and retained as part of the historical artifact.

This book may have occasional imperfections such as missing or blurred pages, poor pictures, errant marks, etc. that were either part of the original artifact, or were introduced by the scanning process. We believe this work is culturally important, and despite the imperfections, have elected to bring it back into print as part of our continuing commitment to the preservation of printed works worldwide. We appreciate your understanding of the imperfections in the preservation process, and hope you enjoy this valuable book.

B. O. BAKER
LAWYER
DALLAS, TEXAS

Exercises
on the
Grammalogues and Contractions
of
Pitman's Shorthand

LAWYER
DALLAS, TEXAS

BY

J. F. C. GROW

LONDON
SIR ISAAC PITMAN & SONS, LTD., 1 AMEN CORNER, E.C.
BATH: PHONETIC INSTITUTE
NEW YORK: 2 WEST 45TH STREET
MELBOURNE: THE RIALTO, COLLINS STREET

TORONTO, CANADA
THE COMMERCIAL TEXT BOOK CO.
OR
THE COPP, CLARK CO., LTD.

PRINTED BY SIR ISAAC PITMAN & SONS, LTD., LONDON, BATH, NEW YORK AND MELBOURNE

Accessions No.
Z56
G91e

Ordered

Of

Received

Invoice

Cost

NOT RUSH WRITE LEGIBLY

Author Inverted: Grow, J F C

Title: Exercises on the grammalogues and contractions of Pitman's shorthand.

No. of Copies ______ Edition ______ Place ______

Publisher ______ Publication date 1915?

Est. Net

Vols. ______ List Price ______ Handling ______

Recommended by ______ Countersigned by ______

to be charged to Library Fund.

UNIVERSITY OF CALIFORNIA, LOS ANGELES

PAGE
. . . v
. . . 7
. . . 18
. . . 32
TICALLY . . . 34

CONTENTS

PAGE

INTRODUCTION v

EXERCISES IN TYPE 7

EXERCISES IN SHORTHAND 18

GRAMMALOGUES PHONETICALLY ARRANGED 32

GRAMMALOGUES AND CONTRACTIONS ALPHABETICALLY ARRANGED 34

TUTTLE JAN 8 '43 LIBRARY SETS

INTRODUCTION

It is admitted by all practical writers of Pitman's Shorthand that one of the important factors in the taking and transcribing of shorthand notes is a perfect knowledge of the logograms and contractions. The exercises in this volume are intended for the purpose of assisting shorthand-writers in this direction.

There are several ways in which the exercises can be used—

(1) The shorthand forms excellent reading practice, and there is no better test of a knowledge of the logograms and contractions than the reading of sentences mainly composed of such outlines.

(2) The type portion may be transcribed into shorthand, and the shorthand portion referred to as a key.

(3) The shorthand may be copied, and such a practice not only fixes the logograms and contractions in the mind, but it is also a splendid aid to the development of a neat and rapid style of writing.

(4) Teachers may dictate the exercises, and then students can check their efforts by means of the shorthand. With this end in view the exercises are marked in divisions of tens. It is suggested that this dictation be given at varying rates, and especially to speed students.

(5) A good plan to adopt is as follows—

Give the students the letters A from the alphabetically-arranged grammalogues and contractions for homework, and the following week dictate the sentences under the letter A. Students should then read back from their own notes, or check their effort from the shorthand. In sixteen weeks, or less where more than one meeting weekly, the whole of the grammalogues and contractions could be revised with very little effort on the part of the students, and without materially interfering with the working of other exercises. If necessary, two or more letters could be given at a time.

In all these ways the exercises should do something to overcome the weaknesses shown by some shorthand-writers in the memorising of the logograms and contractions.

As a means of memorising the logograms there is no better way than taking them phonetically, and for this purpose the list of grammalogues, arranged phonetically, should prove of great value. The alphabetic lists of grammalogues and contractions are included for purposes of reference.

EXERCISES ON THE GRAMMALOGUES AND CONTRACTIONS

A.

The letters of administration enabled the administrator and administratrix to | acknowledge the documents, but the abstraction of the administrator after | the acknowledgment of the papers led to the abandonment of | the enterprise, and although they had all been properly acknowledged | according to law and were of advantage some time ago, | yet by reason of the above circumstance they were not | able to apply themselves to the task and approve subsequent | documents and proceed to administrate. They were slow to acknowledge | the position in which they found themselves, but they ought | to have looked at the consequences in the beginning, as | any good business man would do.

The administrative authority was | vested in the administrator and administratrix, and when they wished | to secure some agricultural land for the purpose of engaging | in the business of agriculture they inserted an advertisement in | the paper to the effect that they would amalgamate their | interests ; but in the course of a few weeks they | were altogether unprepared to carry out the amalgamation. This was | antagonistic to the other side and the matter was submitted | to arbitration, but as they were unable to arbitrate, the | appointment of a receiver followed. As he acted in an | arbitrary manner and would not listen to anything applicable to | the case, much antagonism followed on the part of the | arbitrator and the arbitrament was dropped.

The archbishop was deeply | interested in his work, and when the building of the | Church of the Atonement was contemplated, he engaged an architect | for the attainment of his object and examined many architectural | designs and proceeded with the erection of the edifice ; and | although the architect was aristocratic and the parishioners were of | the aristocracy, yet, to the astonishment of the members of | the Church, the expense was too great and it was | found necessary to make an assignment which certainly was not | auspicious. (311)

B.

The religious services were followed by the baptism of many | men and women into the Baptist Church, including a few | benevolent persons who desired the minister in his benevolence to | baptise them before he baptised other converts who were perhaps | of a more benignant nature. The bondsman and the bondservant, | although of a more lowly station, made vigorous protest with | the result that the church went into bankruptcy. When the | treasurer, on behalf of the congregation proceeded to balance his | books, and had balanced about halfway through, he could foresee | that the balances would not be sufficient because funds had | been abstracted beyond recovery. It was also discovered that they | had started to buy too much land, but it was | then too late to rectify the mistake. (127)

C.

The character of the catholic captain was indicated by the | circumstances of his request for a circumstantial certificate to the | effect that the celestial cabinet were believers in the principles | of Calvinism. One characteristic of the captain was that he | was capable, and in a contingency he could be called | upon to care for the children, teach a child Christianity, | lift a chair with his little finger, engage in commercial | pursuits, cheer the downhearted, maintain his opinions in Christian controversy | and other controversial questions, conduct a cross-examination, cure a cold, | draw up a covenant of warranty, and having cross-examined a | witness he could, under most circumstances, instruct him so that | he could come to an understanding of the Constitution and | live under constitutional law, and he was never known to | put the cart before the horse. (136)

D.

Delinquency in business matters is dangerous, and degeneration of trade | is apt to follow if delinquent customers, who are deficient | in honour or defective in memory, are permitted to contract | debts. It is very dangerous to trust such persons, no | matter what denomination they belong to, until they demonstrate their | ability to pay. A doctor may trust democratic

DALLAS, TE

patients in | the belief that democracy is honourable, and he might feel | secure in denominationalism, but until he has had a demonstration | during many months of their ability and willingness to settle | up, he may pay dear for his confidence. If a | postman should deliver a letter and a merchant make delivery | of goods, if they are delivered promptly it makes little | or no difference how they are delivered ; one is not | different from the other. If we have deliverance from bodily | pain, we say the doctor has done well, and we | put him down as a skilful physician.

There was an | error in the description of the property and it proved | destructive to the transaction. The house was in a dilapidated | condition and had depreciated in value. The owner had difficulty | in money matters, and although he had always carried himself | in a dignified manner and prided himself on his dignity, | yet the destruction of his property caused a dethronement of | his reason and he died a pauper.

The employee was | discharged because of his disinterestedness which caused much displeasure and | disappointment to his parents. His disrespectful manner was disproportionate to | his distinguished birth. His opinions were dissimilar to those of | his father, who wished his son to distinguish himself, but | the doctrine of future punishment had no terrors for him | and he went his own way. (286)

E.

The Englishman was an ecclesiastic authority, and was noted for | his efficiency in all ecclesiastical questions. He was considered the | most efficient clergyman in England, and in every important emergency was | found equal to the occasion. Perhaps in all English-speaking countries | he equalled the best. He was eccentric in his delivery, | and, unlike many ministers, he had made a study of | electricity, and in fact had taken out patents for electrical | devices. His eye was clear and steady, and he was | a bitter foe of all evil.

The Episcopalian clergyman was | an enthusiastic worker and his enthusiasm spread to his parishioners. | He made an especial study of social work, resulting in | the entertainment and enlightenment of his people, and with the | assistance of

James Smith, Esq., who was greatly interested in | church work, he was able to establish social clubs and | thus enlarge the church; and the chancel was also enlarged, | and by this enlargement and the establishment of these various | services everything was brought to a high state of efficiency. |

It is expected that the expenditure for extemporaneous speakers will | prove an expensive proceeding, and may extinguish the funds in | the treasury, and if they should be extinguished by this | action it would certainly prove an extravagant action. The executive | committee, however, which consisted of an executor and executrix, doubted | the expediency of this large expenditure, and upon the exchange | of views among the people the clergyman exchanged pulpits with | a neighbour and thus the large expenditure was avoided. (249)

F—G—H.

The falsification of the books by the accountant, who was, | of course, familiar with the accounts, involved the bank in | financial difficulty last February. This accountant was, of course, quickly | discharged and an assistant whose familiarity with the accounts was | inferior, was obliged to familiarise himself. However, from henceforth the | institution will be governed on more honest lines, and the | new book-keeper will govern himself accordingly. It has generally been | managed with the greatest care for a generation, and the | large quantity of gold stored in the vaults was under | guard of gentlemen who could go on bonds to almost | any amount and had given many of their best years | in the service of the institution. One gentleman said that | he would give a hundred thousand dollars rather than have | the bank fail. Henceforward no fear need be felt.

However | happy a man may think himself, things might happen any | hour, indeed, they have happened to many, to cause him | much misery. The man who appeals to high heaven for | help has a chance to lead a holy life, but | he must know how to keep his house always in | order. (191)

I.

I know the identical location of the store, and if | the manager wishes good business, he must realise the importance | of immediate delivery of his goods, for it is impossible | to make a success if he is accustomed to neglect | his business and fails to make improvements all the time. | It is impracticable to maintain an imperturbable position in an | impregnable fortress and then expect people to come forward and | treat you in a cordial manner. Rather by indefatigable labour | and courtesy, influence customers to come to you and the | improbability of their deserting you will be great.

From information | which I received yesterday I was influenced to try incandescent | lamps in my house. The old candles which I used | were incapable of giving me sufficient light, but the incandescence | from the new light is glorious. The initial cost may | be greater, but a man would on that account be | inconsiderate to ruin his eyes. Besides, the candles are more | inconvenient and the cost should be incorporated in the annual | expenses.

The inscription which was inscribed on the tablet was | inspected by an independent gentleman, and although the inscription represented | the deceased to have been an influential member of society, | yet upon investigation he was informed that the individual in | life had proved himself inefficient and far from indispensable to | his fellows. In fact, his informer stated that his influence | was insignificant, and that his insignificance was a matter of | general knowledge. This information, although contrary to the inscription itself, | was full of instruction to those of his acquaintances who | had always looked upon him as a man of character. |

An inspection of the school led to the discovery of | insubordination on the part of the scholars, and it was | deemed necessary to increase the staff, which seemed to be entirely | insufficient for the insurance of correct behaviour. The intelligence of | the teachers was unquestioned and they could make their lessons | intelligible to the intelligent pupils, but the lack of interest | on the part of some of the pupils, and the | fact that others were insubordinate, led to an investigation by | the school authorities who were interested in the matter and | the introduction of different methods of instruction.

The investment made | by the administrator of the funds left by the ironmonger | proved to be a poor one and was irrecoverable. It | was irregular in its nature, and, irrespective of the fact | that the administrator was a temperance man, he was irresponsible | in a fiduciary capacity, but for some reason or other | he was irremovable from this position; nevertheless, his irresponsibility caused | him to be regarded as uninfluential in his community. (439)

J—K—L.

The knowledge of jurisprudence is most useful in the jurisdiction | of the court, but a knowledge of journalism does not | necessarily effect an entrance into the Kingdom of Heaven. I | do not know exactly how it occurred, but in January | a yellow journal accomplished a journalistic feat of a shady | character, without the knowledge of other papers, which largely increased | its revenues which were already large, and perhaps larger than | those of any paper in the city. The justification for | the story was due to the liberty of the press | and some of the language used could not be found | in the word of the Lord. (106)

M.

The manuscript on the subject of magnetism was prepared for | the monthly magazine, and the manufacturer gave a description of | the wonders of magnetic influence and the manufacture of machines | which he said he had manufactured in Germany many years | ago.

A marconigram is a message transmitted through space by | a mechanical instrument at a maximun speed of lightning. Mr. | Marconi must be credited with the invention. I myself do | not know him, nor does he know me, but as | a member of the same society I hope we may | arrange a meeting at some future time. He has probably | met more people than a mere handful, and it is | my earnest wish that not much time shall pass before | I see him. An ordinary messenger, although of a melancholy | appearance, may be a mathematical genius and become a noted | mathematician.

Methodism in the metropolitan district may have the misfortune | to be grossly misrepresented, but the ministration of the ministry | is so benignant in its nature that it is monstrous | to misrepresent this branch of religion, and it should be | considered a misdemeanour, the minimum punishment for which should be | a union with some monstrosity and an exhibition in a | minstrel show. It should be as much a misdemeanour as | for a man to mortgage property which he does not | own. (221)

N.

The soldier, who was a nonconformist, never failed to proclaim | his adherence to the tenets of nonconformity, and notwithstanding his | neglect of business, he did nothing to violate his vows, | but, nevertheless, during the next month of November, near | the northern boundary of the State, from his natural tendency, | he neglected a number of the practices which naturally belong | to that faith. (63)

O.

The original objection to the organisation was somewhat clouded in | obscurity, but the observation that the objective point of orthodoxy | was the overthrowing of infidelity met with favour, and an | orthodox society was organised by a professional organiser with the | object of clearing away the obstruction to true faith and | to organise society on a higher level, and thus eliminate | obstructive elements.

There is often an opportunity to change the | opinions of oneself, and whatever other men may say, we | ought to study ourselves over and over again and try | to find out of our own volition whether, owing to | their selfishness, we owe anything to our neighbour. (108)

P—Q.

Parliament performs peculiar functions of a parliamentary nature, one peculiarity | of which was to license the performance of a passenger | on the Northern Railway who, as a first-class performer on | the trapeze, performed many daring feats which other passengers were | unable to perform.

The plaintiff, who was a phonographer, not | only took phonographic notes of lectures while standing in a | perpendicular position, but he was widely known as a philanthropist | engaged in philanthropic works, for which he was even commended |

from the platform. He viewed society with a clear perspective, | and his philanthropy was a subject of admiration and commendation. |

The prerogative of a plenipotentiary is practically to remove prejudicial | notions which he encounters in the discharge of the duties | of his high office, and whenever practicable in their preliminary | stages his practice is to warn opponents who have practised | their profession as much as five years that they endeavour | to remove prejudice in every practical way.

The probability is | that a proficient Presbyterian would in all probability desire the | preservation of Presbyterianism, and his adherence to this desire in | his professional capacity would probably be productive of good results, | and it is probable that his proficiency would be thus | enhanced.

The interest of the public in the publication of | the book, a prospectus of which had been already advertised, | was published far and wide as well as the prospective | profits to be derived therefrom. The prospect of the ultimate | success of the project was entertained by the publisher and | by a large proportion of the citizens, who took a | proportionate interest in the stock of the corporation which was | formed to publish the book. The stock was proportionately distributed | and the enterprise was proficiently advertised, and the duties of | the office were duly proportioned to the respective abilities of | the printers.

One reason why so many people take particular | pleasure in acquiring the principles of Phonography is principally the | acquisition of a short mode of writing, but quite as | much, perhaps, in the fact that it will put them | in a position to earn a livelihood. It is questionable | if they should always remain phonographers merely. (357)

R.

Rather than strive for the reformation of criminals, it would | seem to be better that the reformer should endeavour to | reform grafting politics in the city, and after that system | has been reformed seek the regeneration of imprisoned criminals on | their own recognizance, and rather before than after their escape | from prison.

The remarkably clever apprehension of a thief by | a policeman in the course of his regular duties was | witnessed in the avenue to-day, but the remarkable strength of | the captive caused the policeman to relinquish his hold on | the thief, who gave a marvellous representation of fleetness of | foot—at least so the papers represented the affair—whereupon | the policeman remarked that whatever might be his religion or | his religious views, he would remember it for all time ; | and after all, the booty was not recovered and the | policeman could not even remonstrate with him.

With all due | respect to the Republic, the resignation of the republican representative | was repugnant to the best interests of the party, and | the repugnance thus created was represented by the withdrawal by | the citizens of their further support.

The Rev. William Wilkins, | a respected clergyman of the Episcopalian Church and holding a | responsible charge in an important city which was in receipt | of a large revenue, recognising his responsibility, preached to Jews | and Gentiles respectively a sermon more or less retrospective in | its nature, and containing references to the resurrection, which his | respective hearers listened to with interest. (246)

S.

The satisfaction which a sensible man can ecure from selfish | deeds is not clearly understood by a man with a | nature of high sensibility and generous instincts, who cannot believe | that any satisfactory moral results can be obtained from a | life given to selfishness. The fact that sometime in the | future he intends to make a large contribution to charity | is no signification that he has experienced a change of | heart.

It is singular that the stranger who wanted to | do something of a subjective nature subscribed a round sum | to an enterprise relating to the subject of building a | library, for that would be of an objective nature, but | one explanation of the matter was that he was under | subjection to the will of the President of the institution. |

The subscription received was of a sufficient amount to erect | a substantial library building. It was substantially furnished by the | citizens, and for a time was used as a substitute | for the church which had been destroyed by fire, so | that at times the library was turned into a church, | but the sufficiency of the building for either purpose was | never questioned.

The stringency of the money market subjected the | trustees of the school to the practice of economy in | their expenditures. To the surprise of the citizens the strength | of the bank was weakened, and its possible failure was | the subject of the town's talk. They were, however, somewhat | surprised by the significant remark of a wealthy citizen who | suggested that he would advance a hundred thousand dollars if | other citizens would raise fifty thousand dollars. They promised to | consider the suggestion seriously and make special efforts to raise | the amount, and they felt sure that the desired result | could be secured in a short time. A few other | sympathetic men of means signified their willingness to assist, and | in a united spirit the bank was saved. The president | of the bank, who lived in a southern part of | the town, desired to speak specially to his public spirited | neighbours, and sent for them to meet him at the | Town Hall. He complimented them and thanked them, and said | their action reminded him of the remark of the Saviour | in Holy Scripture, "Whatsoever thy hand findeth to do, do | it with thy might." (384)

T.

The thankful parishioners, who were friends of the minister, met | together in the tabernacle for their Thanksgiving service. During that | service a telegraphic message was received by the minister in | the shape of a night telegram, telling him that the | Board of Trade had passed a resolution thanking him for | what he had done for them in presenting the truth | on two occasions. The minister read this to those who | were assembled in the tabernacle with him, and they all | agreed that he was a public spirited citizen and a | true friend, and they would thenceforward try through all his | ministry to help him in his work. He proceeded to | tell them how much he appreciated their kindness. The subject | of transubstantiation, in regard to which they held dissimilar views, | was referred to a tribunal for investigation. It was then | getting towards twelve o'clock, and the minister therefore dismissed them | with his blessing, and thus ended a very satisfactory meeting. | (160)

U—V.

The bill, although generally considered unconstitutional, was passed unanimously, and | by the unanimous consent of all who understood the question, | the resolution of the House was read and passed. Many | could not understand the unexampled uniformity with which it was | acted upon. The Senate unexpectedly voted it down as it | was believed to have been unconstitutionally passed by the House | but, as is often the case, the unexpected happened.

The | unquestionable character of the place was uniformly accepted. The uniform | consideration of the uninteresting question by the members of the | club in an unselfish spirit was unquestionably a criterion of | the unselfishness of the members. The lack of uniformity by | an uninfluential body of men on a simple question of | benefit to the people in general, indicated that their deliberations | were unsatisfactory and unsubstantial.

The practice of eating nothing but | vegetables is called vegetarianism, and one who abstains from eating | meat is a vegetarian. If vegetarianism were a universal practice | it would in a very short time reduce the price | of beef. The majority of people, of course, are unsympathetic | concerning the custom, and the universality of vegetarianism will probably | never be brought about. There are some students in the | university who believe that the universe was created for their | special benefit, but they are doubtless unprincipled, although some of | the students are upright citizens and believe in Universalism, and | some of them place a very high valuation upon the | doctrine of that creed. (244)

W—Y.

Whensoever a question of a philosophic nature arises, philosophers should | endeavour to explain it whereinsoever they may differ or wheresoever | it may arise, or whithersoever it may lead. Young men | and youths, as well as old philosophers, should philosophise on | such questions year in and year out, even though they | may be a yard apart or miles apart in their | understanding of the subject. (64)

A.

B.

C.

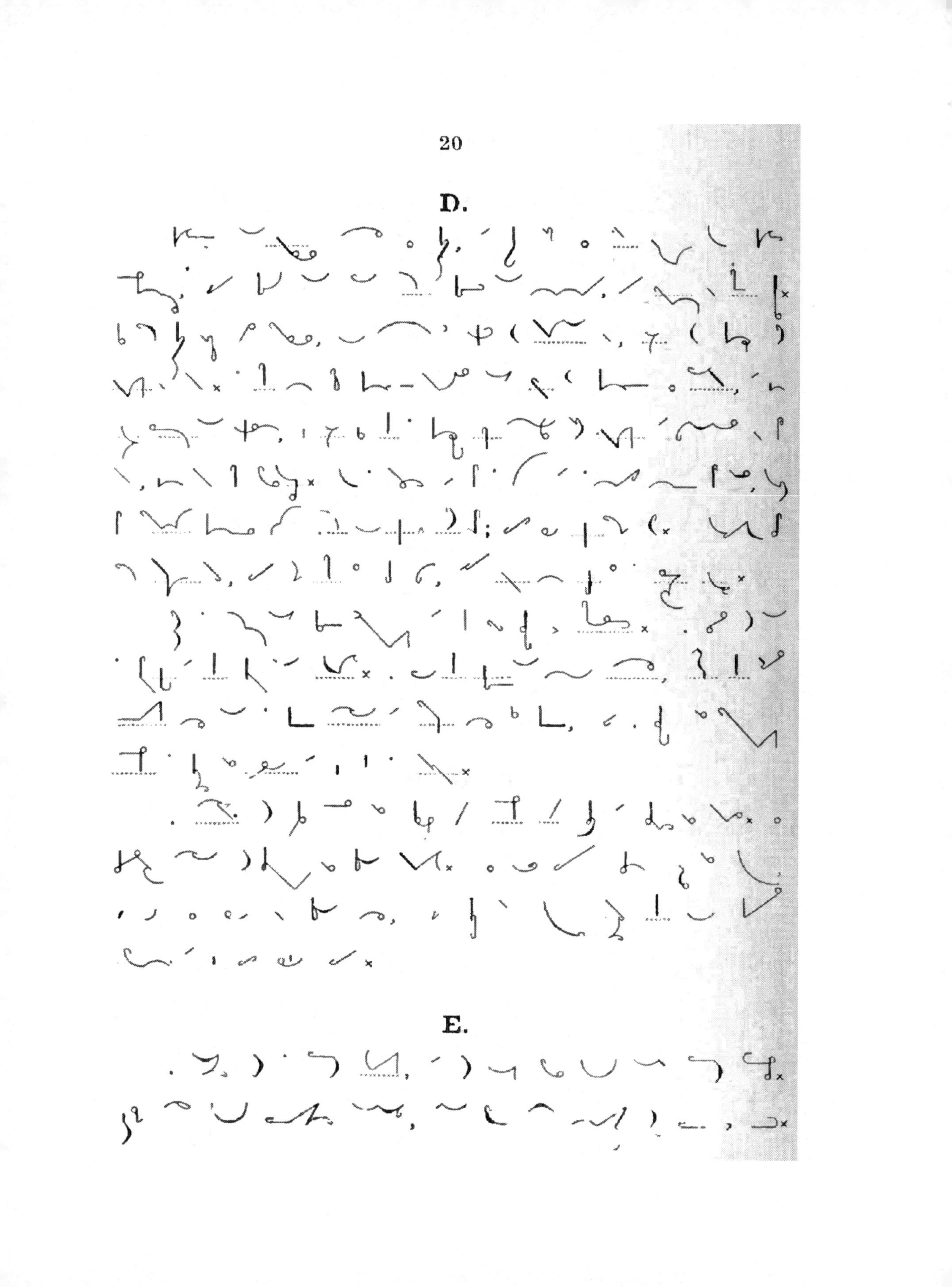

D.

E.

F—G—H.

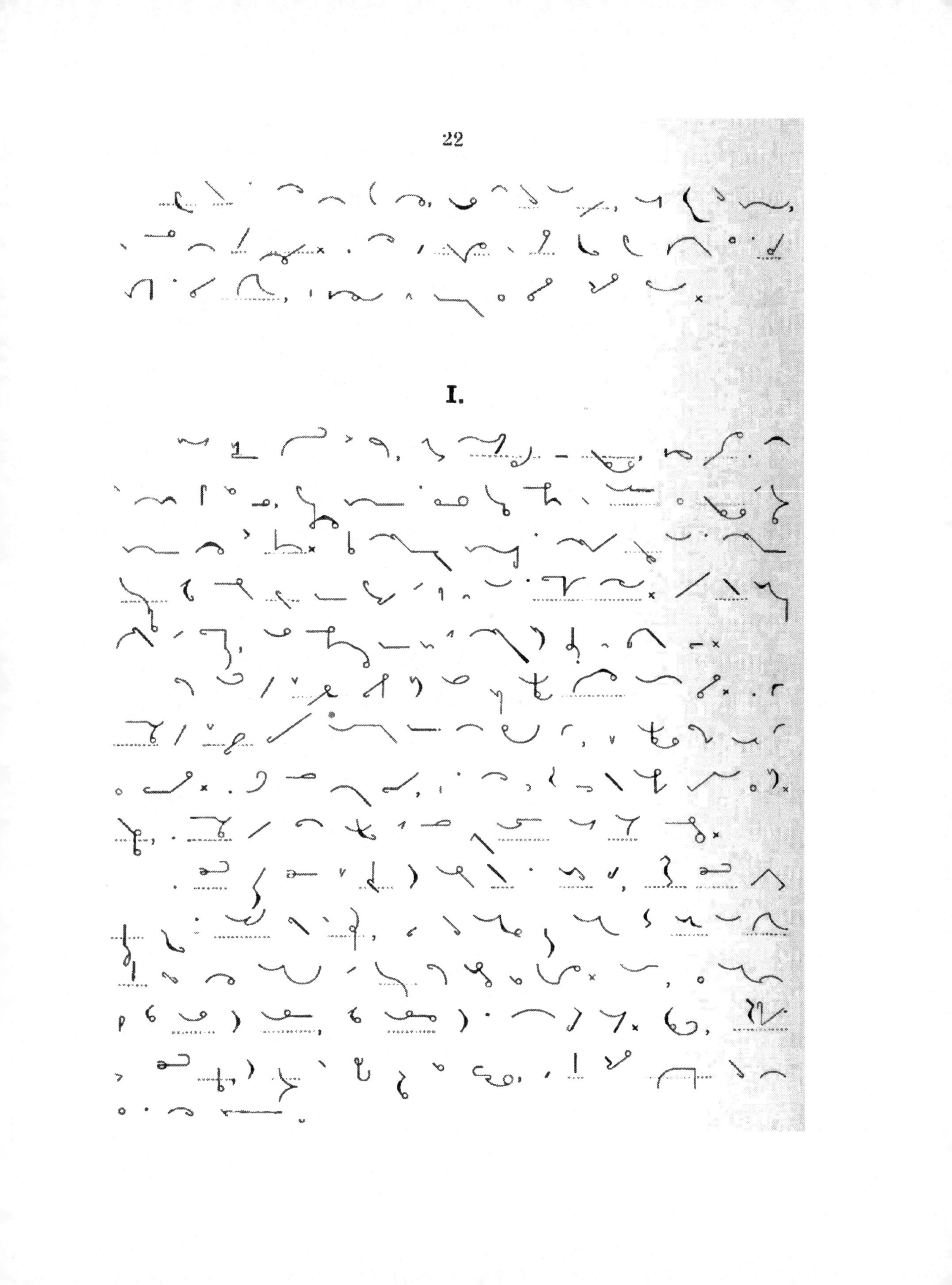

I.

J—K—L.

M.

N.

O.

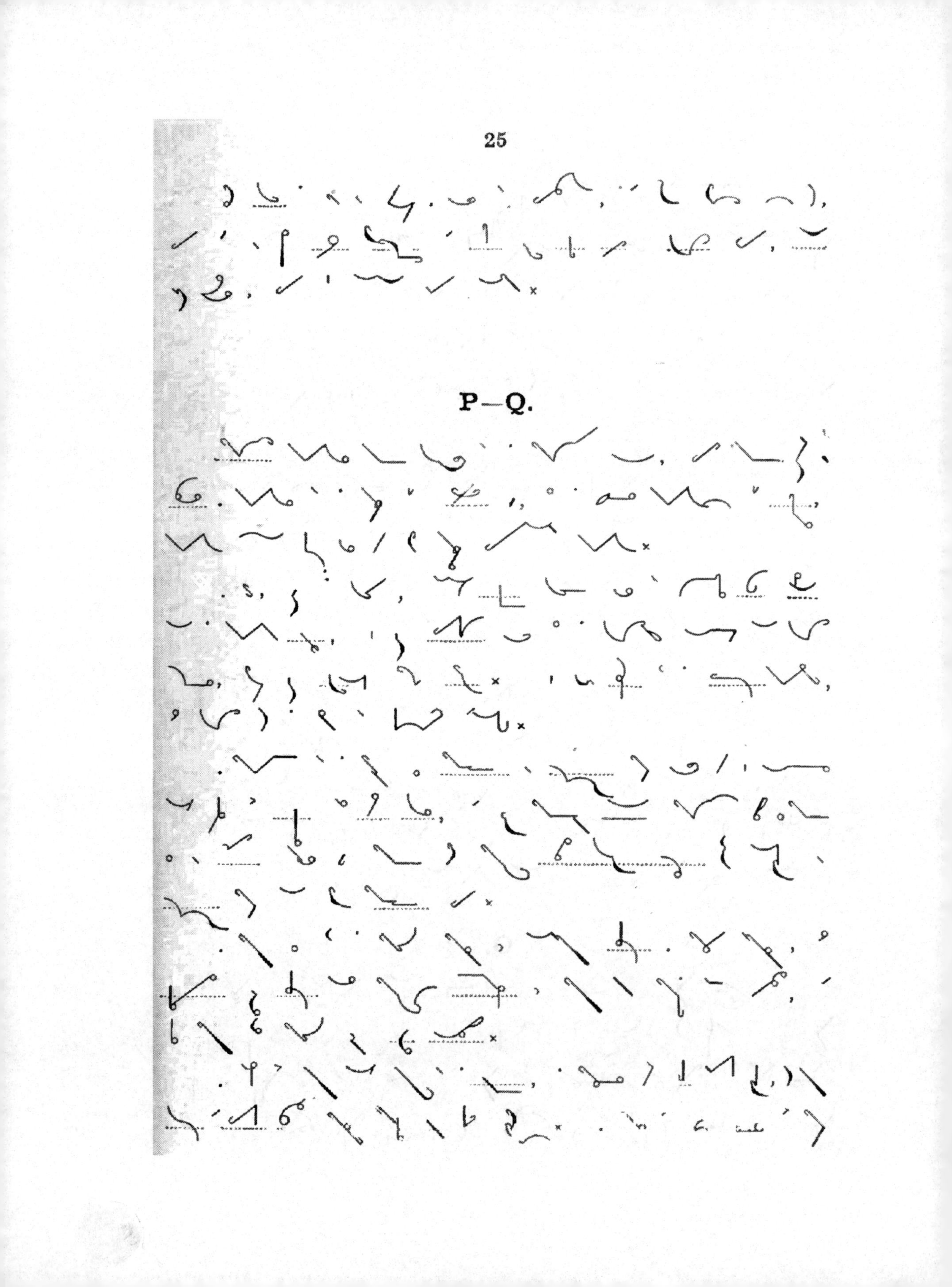

P—Q.

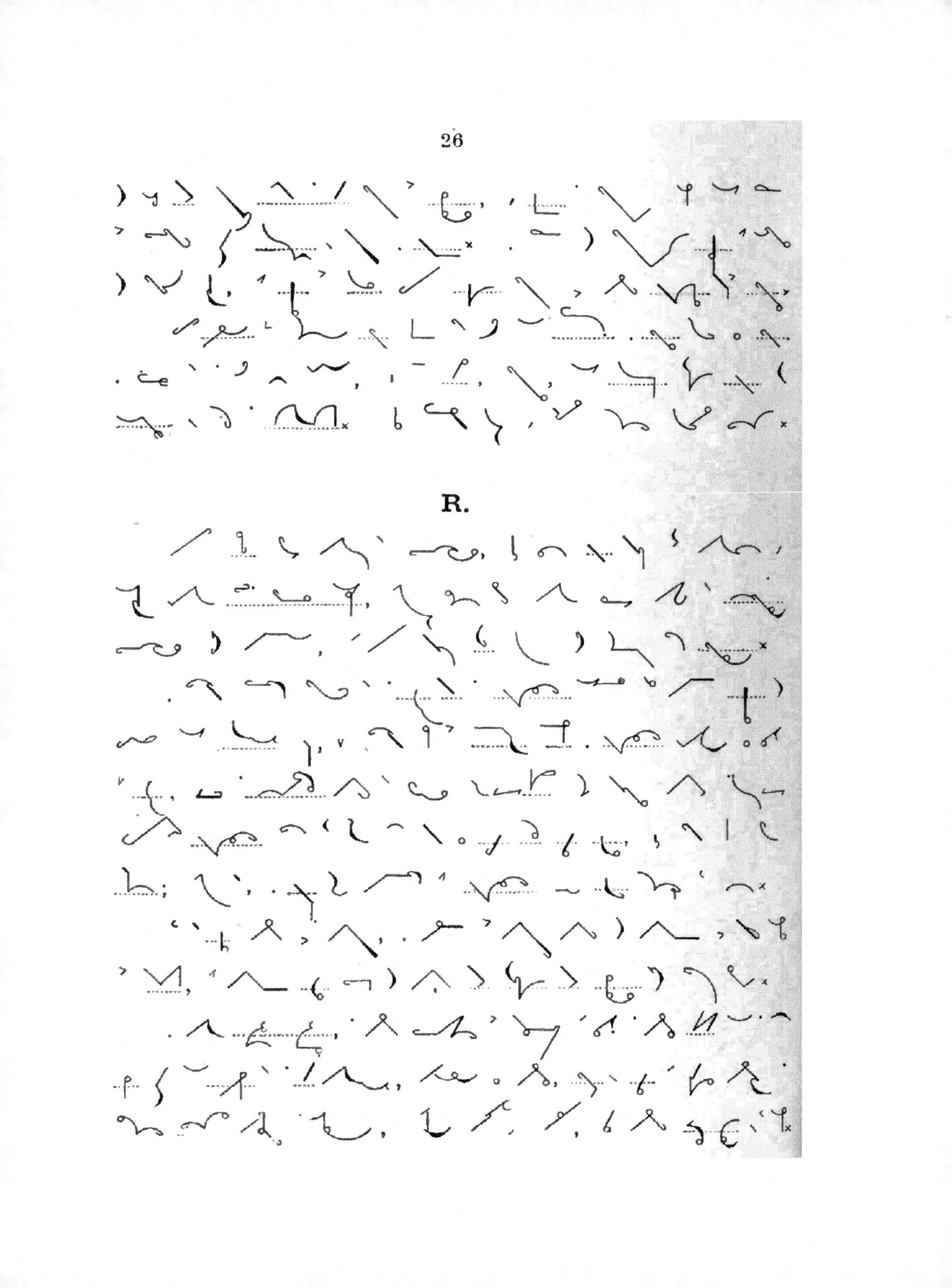

R.

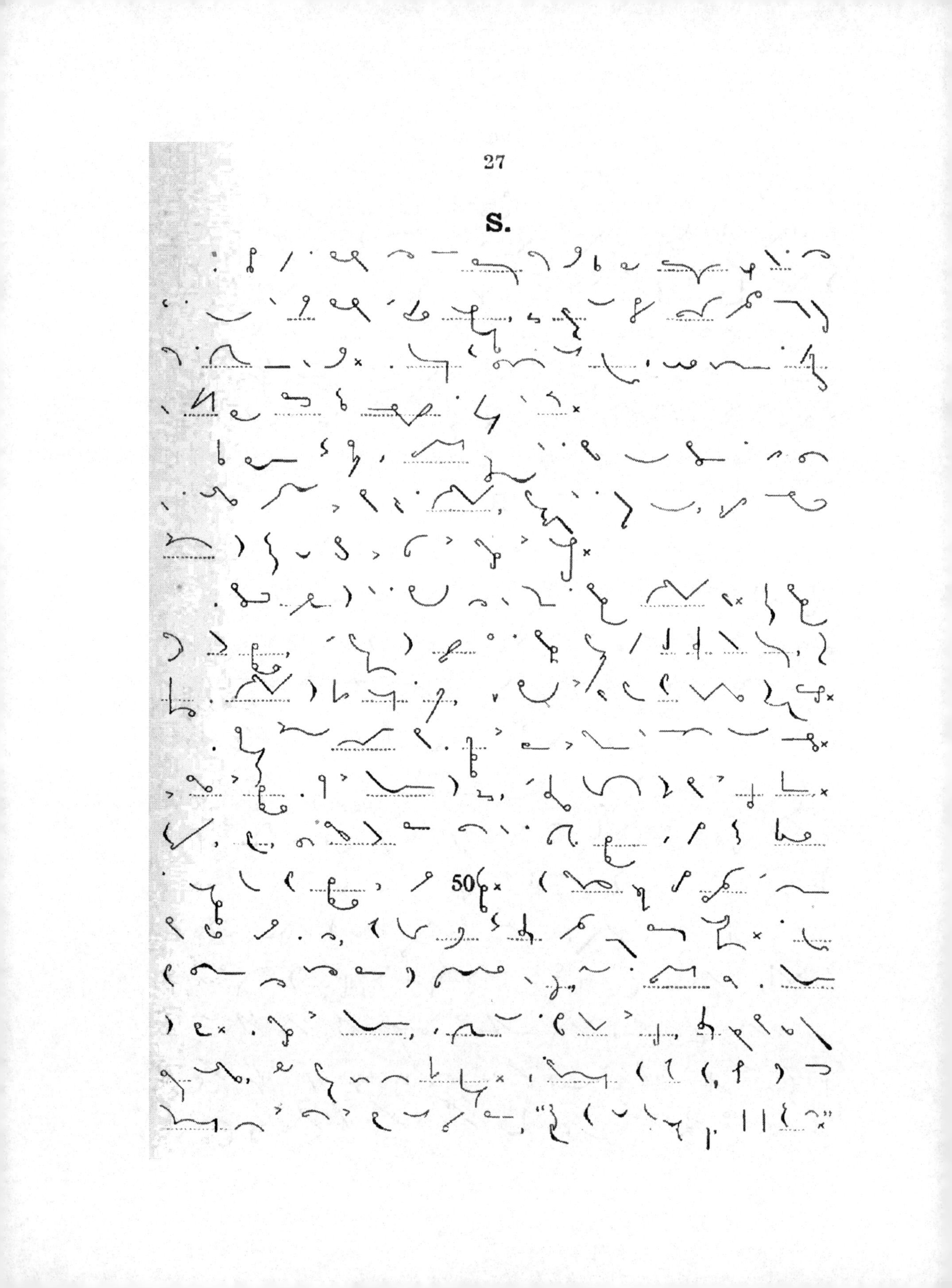

S.

50

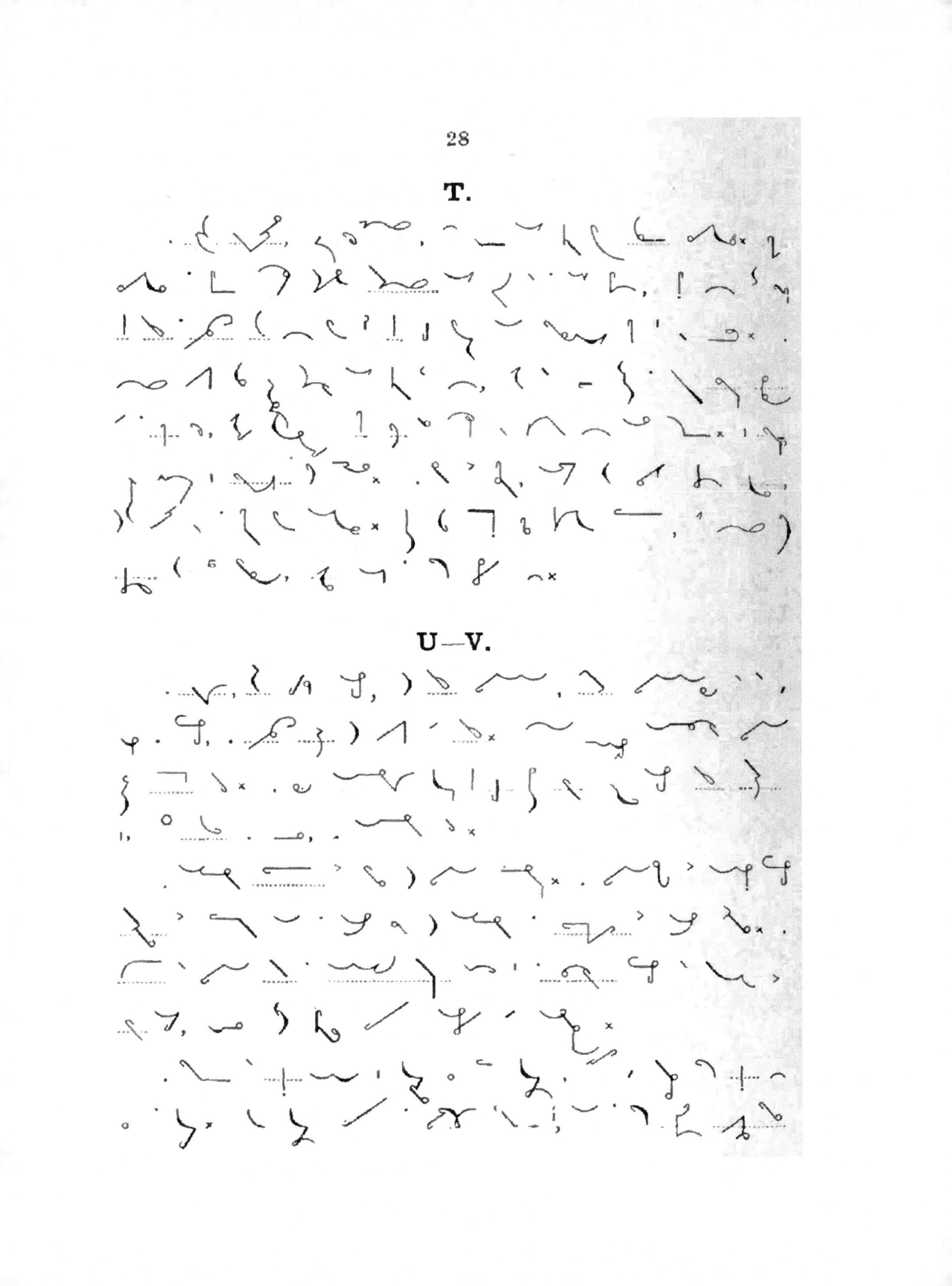

T.

U—V.

W—Y.

Grammalogues and Contractions

Grammalogues

PHONETICALLY ARRANGED

CONSONANTS.

1 happy, 2 up, 3 put
1 happen, 2 upon
1 happened
1 apply, 3 people
3 principle, principal-ly
1 particular, 2 opportunity
1 approve
1 surprise
1 surprised

1 by, buy, 2 be, 3 to be
2 subject-ed
2 subjective
2 subjection
1 behalf, 2 above
2 been
2 able, 3 belief, believe-d
1 balance
1 balances
1 balanced
2 build-ing
1 liberty, 2 member, remember-ed, 3 number-ed

1 at, 2 it, 3 out
3 itself
2 tell, 3 till
2 told
1 try, 2 truth, 3 true
1 tried, 2 trade, 2 towards

1 had, 2 do, 3 different-ence
2 did
1 advantage, 3 difficult
2 done, 3 down
2 deliver-ed-y
2 deliverance
1 Dr. 2 dear, 3 during

1 much, 2 which 3 each
1 child
3 children
2 chair, 3 cheer
1 chaired, 2 cheered

1 large
2 suggest-ed
2 suggestion
2 suggestive
3 religious
2 justification
2 general-ly, 3 religion
2 generalization
1 gentleman, 2 gentlemen
1 largely
1 larger, 2 journal
2 generation

1 can, 2 come
1 quite, 2 could
1 because
1 cannot
1 call, 2 equal-ly
1 called, 2 cold, equalled
1 Christian, Christianity
2 care
1 accord-ing, cart, 2 cared

1 go, ago, 2 give-n
2 gold
1 guard, 2 great
2 greatest

1 half, 2 if
1 often, 2 Phonography
2 for
2 from

2 have
2 heaven
1 over, 2 ever-y, 3 however
2 very
1 valuation, 3 evil

1 thank-ed, 2 think, 3 youth
3 through, threw
2 third

1 though 2 them, they
1 that, 2 without
1 those, thyself, 2 this, 3 thus, these, youths
2 themselves
3 within
2 southern
2 other
2 there, their
3 therefore

1 has, as, 2 his, is
1 saw, 2 so, us, 3 see, sea
2 first
2 special-ly, 3 speak
2 spirit
2 satisfaction
2 circumstance
2 circumstances
2 strength
2 instruction
2 instructive
1 Scripture
2 secret
2 school
2 schooled
1 inscribe-d
1 inscription
1 signify-ied-ficant
1 significance
1 signification
2 several, Saviour
1 sent
2 somewhat

2 was, 3 whose

2 shall, shalt, 3 wish
2 selfish-ness
2 initial-ly-ed
3 sure
1 short

2 usual-ly
2 pleasure

1 me, my, 2 him, may
1 met, 2 meeting
1 myself, 2 himself
1 most, 2 must

1 important-ance, 2 improve-ed-ment
1 impossible, 2 improvesments
1 more, remark-ed, 2 Mr. mere

1 in, any, 2 no, know, 3 own
1 influence
1 influenced, 2 next
1 not
1 hand, 2 under
1 information
2 opinion
1 nor, 2 near
1 northern

1 language, owing, 2 thing, 3 young

2 Lord

2 are, 3 our, hour
3 ourselves
1 rather, writer
1 or, 2 your, 3 year
1 yard, 2 word

2 we, way
2 one
2 wonderful-ly
2 will

2 whether, 3 whither
1 while

2 yes

1 high
2 holy
2 house

Vowels.

Dots. a, an, the, ah! aye, eh?

Dashes. of, on, and,
all, O, oh! owe, awe, ought, aught
to, but, should
two, too, who.

Diphthongs.

I, eye, ay (yes), how,

with, when, what, would,

beyond, you.

Grammalogues.

A

a *or* an
able
above
accord-ing
advantage
ago
ah !
all
and
any
apply
approve
are
as
at
aught
awe
ay (yes)
aye

B

balance
balanced
balances
be
because
been
behalf
belief-ve-d
beyond
build-ing
but
buy
by

C

call
called
can
cannot
care
cared
cart
chair
chaired
cheer
cheered
child
children
Christian-ity
circumstance
circumstances
cold
come
constitutional-ly
could

D

dear
deliver-ed-y
deliverance
difference-t
difficult
do
doctor, Dr.
done
down
during

E

each
eh ?
equal-ly
equalled
ever-y
evil
eye

F

first
for
from

G

general-ly
generalization
generation
gentleman
gentlemen
give-n
go
gold
great
greatest
guard

H

had
half
hand
happen
happened
happy
has
have
he
heaven
high
him
himself
his
holy
hour
house
how
however

I

I
if
importance-ant
impossible
improve-d-ment
improves-ments
in
influence
influenced
information
initial-ly-ed
inscribe-d
inscription
instruction
instructive
is
it
itself

J

journal
justification

K

know

L

language
large
largely
larger
liberty
Lord

M

may
me
meeting
member
mere
met
more
most
Mr.
much
must
my
myself

N

near
next
no
nor
northern
not
number-ed

O

O ! oh !
of
often
on
one
opinion
opportunity
or
other
ought
our
ourselves
out
over
owe
owing
own

P

particular
people
phonography
pleasure
principal-ly
principle
put

Q

quite

R

rather
religion

religious
remark-ed
remember-ed

S

satisfaction
Saviour
saw
school
schooled
Scripture
sea
see
selfish-ness
sent
several
shall, shalt
short
should
significance
significant
signification
signify-ied
so
somewhat
southern
speak
special-ly
spirit
strength
subject-ed
subjection
subjective
suggest-ed
suggestion
suggestive
sure
surprise
surprised

T

tell
thank-ed
that
the
their
them
themselves
there
therefore
these
they
thing
think
third
this
those
though
threw
through
thus
thyself
till
to
to be
told
too
towards
trade
tried
true
truth
try
two

U

under
up
upon
us
usual-ly

V

valuation
very

W

was
way
we
what
when
whether
which
while
whither
who
whose
why
will
wish
with
within
without
wonderful-ly
word
would
writer

Y

yard
ye
year
yes
you
young
your
youth
youths

Contractions.

A

abandonment
abstraction
abstractive
acknowledge
acknowledged
acknowledgment
administrate
administration
administrative
administrator
administratrix
advertise-d-ment
agriculture-al
altogether
amalgamate
amalgamation
antagonist-ic-ism
anything
applicable-ility
appointment
arbitrament
arbitrary
arbitrate
arbitration
arbitrator
archbishop
architect-ure-al
aristocracy-atic
assignment
astonish-ed-ment
atonement
attainment
auspicious

B

bankruptcy
baptize-d-st-ism
benevolent-ce
benignant-ity
bondservant
bondsman

C

cabinet
Calvinism
capable
captain
catholic
certificate
character
characteristic
circumstantial
commercial
contentment
contingency
controversy-ial
covenant
cross-examination
cross-examine-d

D

danger
dangerous
defective
deficient-cy
degeneration
delinquency
delinquent
democracy-atic
demonstrate
demonstration
denomination-al
denominational-ism
depreciate-d
depreciatory
description
destruction
destructive
destructively
dethronement
difficulty
dignify-ied-ty
dilapidate-d-ion
disappointment
discharge-d
disinterested-ness
displeasure
disproportion-ed
disproportionate
disrespect
disrespectful
dissimilar
distinguish-ed
doctrine

E

ecclesiastic-al
efficient-cy
electric

electrical
electricity
emergency
England
English
Englishman
enlarge
enlarged
enlargement
enlarger
enlightenment
entertainment
enthusiastic-iasm
Episcopal-ian-ism
especial
esquire
establish-ed-ment
evangelical
everything
exchange-d
executive
executor
executrix
expect-ed
expediency
expenditure
expensive
extemporaneous
extinguish-ed
extraordinary
extravagant-ance

F

falsification
familiar-ity
familiarization
familiarize
February
financial

G

govern-ed
Government

H

henceforth
henceforward
howsoever

I

identical
immediate
imperfect-ion
imperturbable
impracticable
impregnable
improbable-ility
incandescence
incandescent
incapable
inconsiderate
inconvenience-t
incorporated
indefatigable
independent-ce
indescribable
indignant-ion
indiscriminate
indispensable
individual
inefficient-cy
influential
inform-ed
informer
insignificance
insignificant
inspect-ed-ion
insubordinate-ion
insufficient-cy
insurance
intelligence
intelligent
intelligible
interest
interested
introduction
investigation
investment
ironmonger
irrecoverable
irregular
irremovable
irrespective
irrespectively
irresponsible-ility

J

January
journalism
journalistic
jurisdiction
jurisprudence

K

knowledge

L

legislative
legislature

M

magnetic-ism
manufacture-d

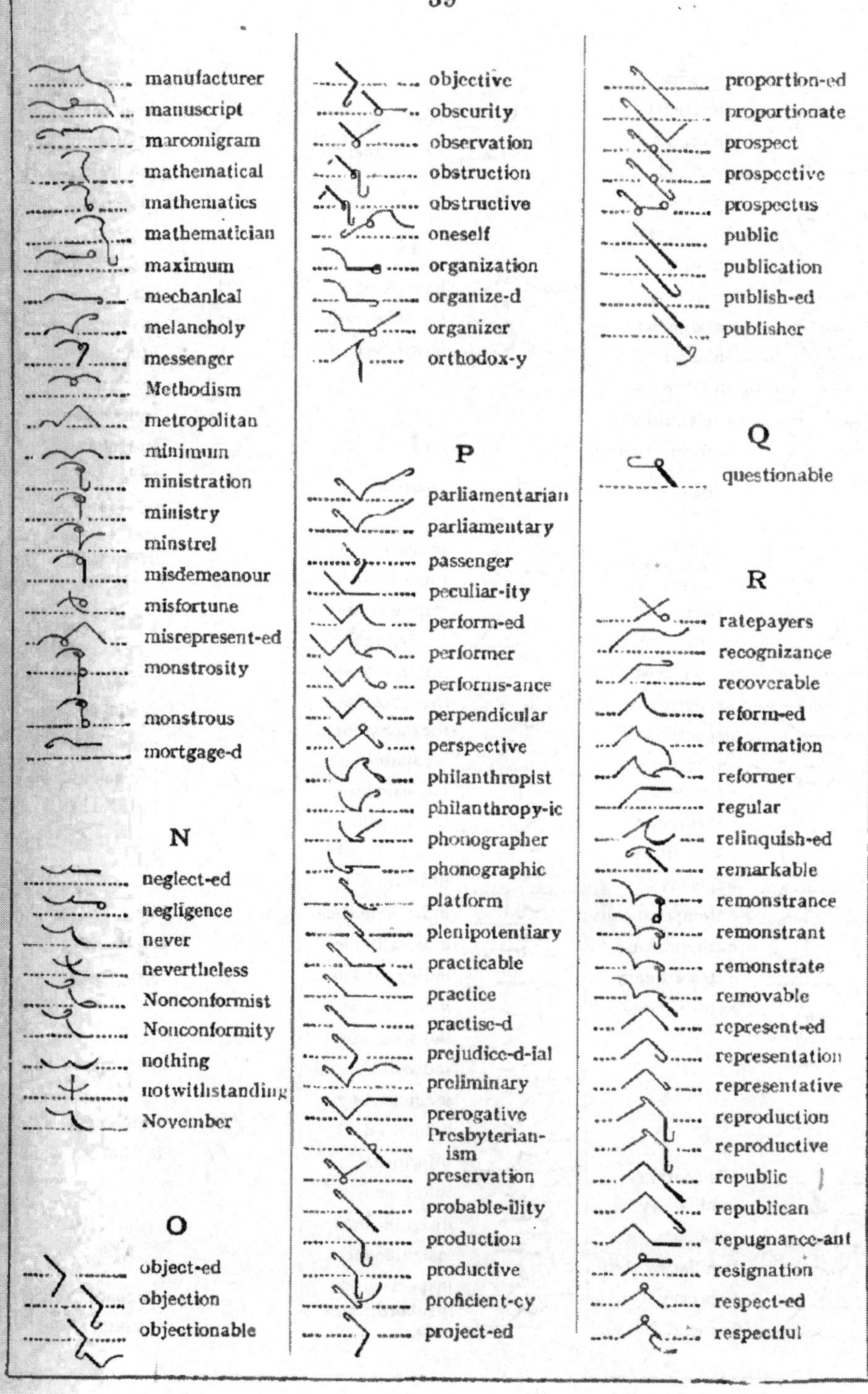

manufacturer
manuscript
marconigram
mathematical
mathematics
mathematician
maximum
mechanical
melancholy
messenger
Methodism
metropolitan
minimum
ministration
ministry
minstrel
misdemeanour
misfortune
misrepresent-ed
monstrosity
monstrous
mortgage-d

N

neglect-ed
negligence
never
nevertheless
Nonconformist
Nonconformity
nothing
notwithstanding
November

O

object-ed
objection
objectionable
objective
obscurity
observation
obstruction
obstructive
oneself
organization
organize-d
organizer
orthodox-y

P

parliamentarian
parliamentary
passenger
peculiar-ity
perform-ed
performer
performs-ance
perpendicular
perspective
philanthropist
philanthropy-ic
phonographer
phonographic
platform
plenipotentiary
practicable
practice
practise-d
prejudice-d-ial
preliminary
prerogative
Presbyterian-ism
preservation
probable-ility
production
productive
proficient-cy
project-ed
proportion-ed
proportionate
prospect
prospective
prospectus
public
publication
publish-ed
publisher

Q

questionable

R

ratepayers
recognizance
recoverable
reform-ed
reformation
reformer
regular
relinquish-ed
remarkable
remonstrance
remonstrant
remonstrate
removable
represent-ed
representation
representative
reproduction
reproductive
republic
republican
repugnance-ant
resignation
respect-ed
respectful

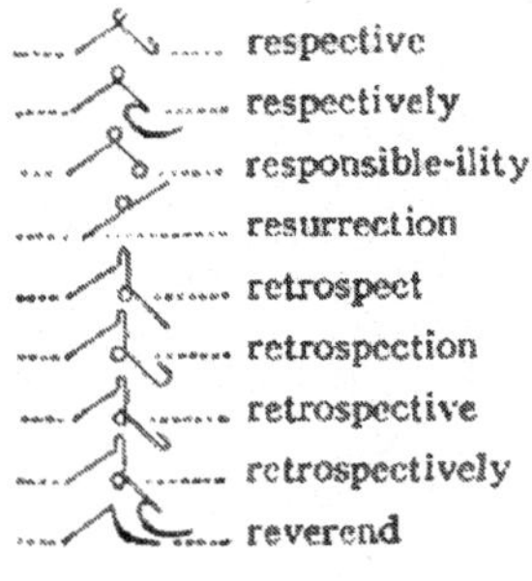

respective
respectively
responsible-ility
resurrection
retrospect
retrospection
retrospective
retrospectively
reverend

S

satisfactory
sensible-ility
singular
something
stranger
stringency
subscribe-d
subscription
substantial
sufficient-cy
suspect-ed
sympathetic

T

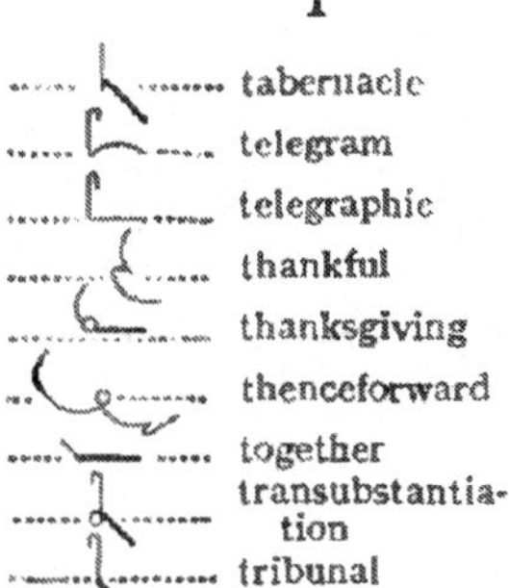

tabernacle
telegram
telegraphic
thankful
thanksgiving
thenceforward
together
transubstantiation
tribunal

U

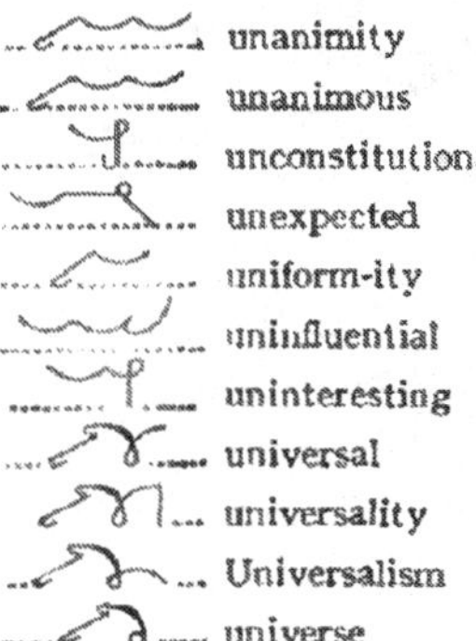

unanimity
unanimous
unconstitutional
unexpected
uniform-ity
uninfluential
uninteresting
universal
universality
Universalism
universe

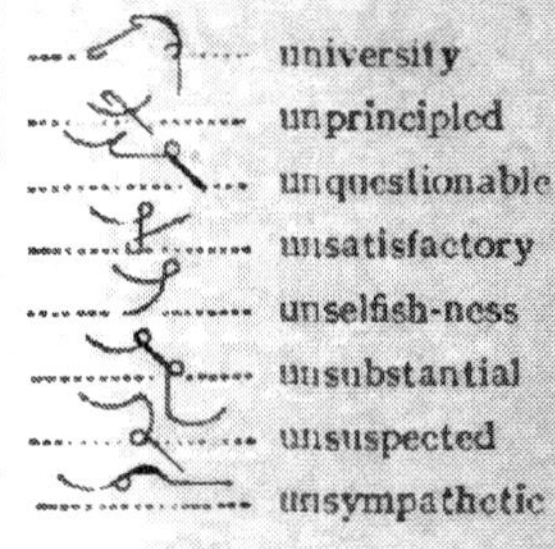

university
unprincipled
unquestionable
unsatisfactory
unselfish-ness
unsubstantial
unsuspected
unsympathetic

V

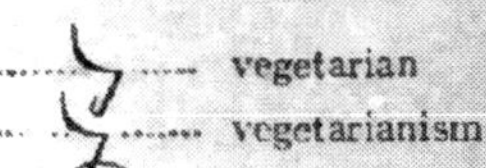

vegetarian
vegetarianism

W

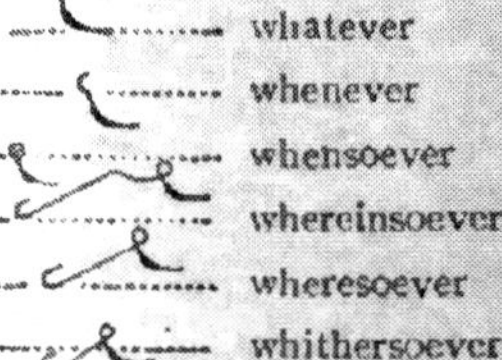

whatever
whenever
whensoever
whereinsoever
wheresoever
whithersoever

Y

yesterday

B. C. [illegible]KER
LAWYER
DALLAS, TEXAS

Printed by Sir Isaac Pitman & Sons, Ltd., Bath.
P5-(170)

B. O. BAKER
LAWYER
DALLAS, TEXAS

CPSIA information can be obtained
at www.ICGtesting.com
Printed in the USA
LVOW03s1326100216
474519LV00014B/447/P